The
Knucklebone
Floor

The Knucklebone Floor

Linda France

Smokestack Books
1 Lake Terrace,
Grewelthorpe,
Ripon
HG4 3BU
e-mail: info@smokestack-books.co.uk
www.smokestack-books.co.uk

Copyright 2022,
Linda France

ISBN 9781838465377

Smokestack Books
is represented by
Inpress Ltd

Susan Davidson (1796?–1877) landscaped her estate at Ridley Hall in Northumberland with 'wilderness walks', introducing stairways, bridges, summerhouses, trees and a tarn onto the site of a dramatic erosion gorge and ancient woodland at Allen Banks. This book is dedicated to her and the other women who worked and walked there during her lifetime, as well as all those before them and we who follow.

SAPIENTER SI SINCERE

IN A VAULT BENEATH THE CHANCEL OF THIS CHAPEL
REST THE REMAINS OF
SUSAN HUSSEY ELIZABETH JESSUP
DAUGHTER OF LADY ANNA MARIA JESSUP
GRANDDAUGHTER OF THE EARL OF STRATHMORE AND
WIDOW OF JOHN DAVIDSON ESQ
LATE OF RIDLEY HALL AND WEST OTTERBURN IN THIS COUNTY
SHE DIED ON THE 11 JUNE 1877 AGED 83
HAVING OUTLIVED HER LATE HUSBAND FOR MORE THAN   YEARS
MUCH ATTACHED TO THE   SHE RESTORED
VERY MANY YEARS AT RIDLEY HALL

PROPERTY   IT WAS HER CONSTANT PLEASURE
TO ADORN AND BEAUTIFY AND SHE NEVER FAILED
TO TAKE THE GREATEST INTEREST
IN THE WELFARE OF HER   WITH HER
IN REMEMBRANCE OF HER   BENEVOLENTLY SPENT
THIS TABLET   AND THE
AND BY HER AFFECTIONATE COUSIN
JOHN BOWES

Contents

I
IN A VAULT

A Hundred Ways to Know Our Place	15
October: Samhain	21
We, the Dead	22
Morralee Wood	23
December: Winter Solstice	26
Signs of Erosion	27
Gorge	28
Botanical Emblem	*Snowdrop*	29

II
PROPERTY

Girlhood	33
Pedigree	35
White Birch and Blackthorn	36
Matrimony	37
February: Imbolc	38
Hurricane	39
Rue d'Angoulême	40
Revêtements	41
Room Outdoors	42
March: Spring Equinox	43
Second Nature	44
Botanical Emblem	*Marsh Marigold*	45

III
HER CONSTANT PLEASURE
TO ADORN AND BEAUTIFY

Revolution	49
Tarn	50
Not Words but Deeds	51
Allen Banks Flora	52
May: Beltane	56
Pedometers for Ladies	57
Unrelated	58
In Praise of the View Across the Valley	59
Written in the Dark	60
sketch for a sonnet, unattributed	61
To Squire Bruno of Ridley Hall	62
Bilberry Hill Moss House	63
Sun on the Cusp of the Bull and Twins	64
The Cedar Hut (Deconstructed)	66
Botanical Emblem	*Mountain Pansy*	67

IV
THE GREATEST INTEREST
IN THE WELFARE

Staffage	71
Seedlip Girls	72
The Shieling	73
June: Summer Solstice	74
Stonepicker	75
Under the Eaves	76
Wild Teasel	77
Pressed Flowers	78
Salvage	79
Lapidary	80
Botanical Emblem	*Throatwort*	81

V
IN REMEMBRANCE OF

Mighty, Far-springer, Queen	85
Unnatural	86
August: Lughnasa	87
Feverish Note	88
Blank	89
Memorandum (Found Among Our Papers)	90
China, blue and white	92
Self-Portrait as a Collective Noun	93
Coup de Théâtre	94
Plenitude	95
September: Autumn Equinox	96
No/Return	97
For Those Unborn	98
Winding Sheet	99
Flock	100
Heartland	102
Botanical Emblem	*Black-Eyed Susan*	103
Notes and References	105
Acknowledgements	112

I
IN A VAULT

A Hundred Ways to Know Our Place

'Our knowledge is not like the learning of men, to be reproduced in some literary composition nor <u>ever</u> in any learned profession, but is to come out in conduct.'

Hannah More

1. We are given the names of flowers, delicate, aromatic – Violet, Lily, Rose.
2. Our family names honour sons, their land and professions. No names for our labour, no territory to call our own.
3. Birches and backboards break us in.
4. We seek to improve ourselves.
5. We sit by a window, drawing down what light we can.
6. We are laced tight.
7. There is blackbird, there is robin, hearts full of singing.
8. We tend forests, glades – ferns and aspidistras in pots, ranged round our rooms on pedestals – trophies, talking points.
9. We need to be small – small as daisies, small as kittens, small as little girls.
10. Come, let's play hide and seek, solitaire, charades.
11. According to Clippity-Clop-Schopenhauer, we are childish, frivolous, short-sighted, by our very nature meant to obey.
12. We stand on the brink of light, brink of dark, dizzy with atmospheres colliding.
13. Taught to be good, we wake up with someone else's voice in our ears.
14. We are brittle with longing and fury.
15. We want to dance in the garden with badly-chosen strangers.

16. In the mirror of Perseus's shield, we wear our hair in coils upon our heads.
17. The creases of our skin are raw and weeping.
18. We read stories about people who aren't us, trace their empty footsteps.
19. Peruse our collection of birds' nests, all the eggs unhatched.
20. We may as well be ghosts.
21. As befits ladies, we do not attend funerals.
22. We sip broth from the sides of silver spoons, flavourless, penitential.
23. Our fathers' daughters, brothers' sisters, husbands' wives, sons' mothers, we are adjunct, footnote, object.
24. Watercolours portray us as daffodils, dahlias, pretty maids all in a row.
25. We do not accept every dish that is offered.
26. In cast-iron beds like leaky boats, damp creeps in to our sleep.
27. We dream of moving earth and channelling water.
28. We are hardly mistresses of our own pantries.
29. Our cheeks are peaches, unless they're stones.
30. We hold out our hands to women falling, children bundled against the cold air of their descent.
31. We are spider and cobweb and fly.
32. Silence is unacceptable, the wrong sort of conversation objectionable.
33. What colour should we paint patience?
34. Our language is The Queen's English, written or spoken, never vulgar.
35. We find ourselves sending many letters – thanks, congratulation, condolence.
36. We are alone and given to countless fictions.

37. We use good black ink; pale ink inexcusable; blue ink dangerous, a fathomless ocean when wet.
38. We are invisible.
39. We drag our bodies around in cages.
40. Our gardens are planted with lurid displays of Hysteria, Dyspepsia, Neuralgia.
41. Our words do not echo our thoughts. We tumble to our deaths in the canyons between them.
42. Not acknowledged until presented at Court, no, when we will be dressed all in white.
43. We are always falling, always autumn.
44. We are not sweet, pretty or modest as the earth we're made of is ditto etc etc.
45. Bonfires crackle inside us.
46. We have a terror of abandonment.
47. We eat bread and butter, rolled up, occasionally cake, with our tea.
48. We do not smoke.
49. We keep lists of visitors in books, like accountants. Calls are made between the hours of four and seven. Our dogs are never welcome – our ever-faithful, forgiving dogs.
50. We are trained to be firm but fair with our servants, though they plague us.
51. Some days our faces show what's on the inside and everyone is exasperated.
52. We listen to water to be close to our mothers.
53. We do not appear to advantage if we try to imitate the opposite sex. It elicits an awkward attention.
54. We must accord our husbands a freedom it is not their duty to offer us.
55. Our fathers, brothers, guardians give us away.

56. Moulding ourselves to the circumstances and characters of our beloved husbands, their happiness and fidelity remain our responsibility.
57. Our bouquets are pure white – camellias, azaleas, stephanotis, sprays of orange blossom.
58. It is our task to submerge our individual preferences and endeavour to promote the greatest good for the greatest number of souls.
59. We embroider it on our samplers – *We must not look at goblin men. We must not buy their fruit.*
60. Our dressing tables are altars, fit for our transformation into saints, into angels.
61. We cleave to our children who die in our arms, in their beds, in rivers, in baskets, on doorsteps.
62. Ashes of roses and sage green: carpets, upholstery and curtains muffle any noises no one would wish to hear.
63. *Help us, O Lord our God, for we rest on thee.*
64. We are magpies, hoarding Chinoiserie, cloisonné, manufactured ceramic, lacquer.
65. In our opulent nests, we are starved.
66. For unmentionable reasons, we no longer bleed. We also bleed.
67. We are sequestered in the wings of houses, cloistered at the end of corridors, immured in attics.
68. Our rooms so packed, we lose ourselves among the bric-a-brac.
69. We are kept busy doing nothing, forever and ever. Amen.
70. We rarely immerse ourselves in water, hot or cold.
71. Leaf by leaf, we count the acanthus embossed on the wallpaper.
72. We cry. We try not to cry. There is silence.
73. We have our favourite chairs, those that show our best sides.

74. Our hearths inadequate, we are chilled to the bone.
75. We are the Daughters of Innocence, the Sisters of Shame.
76. We stay on guard against Satan.
77. Our passions, our disobedience, our idleness are errors, to be swiftly corrected.
78. Our nightmares slip in beside us so our dreams stay a long way off.
79. We are spinsters, who never patched a child from our yarn.
80. We struggle to keep our countenance.
81. We must never grow old.
82. Nor need we be 'New', asking for what we want, stating our case.
83. Never breathe a word of politics.
84. Too much reading induces the deplorable growth of our noses, the withering of our breasts.
85. We draw portraits of each other that look like ourselves.
86. We might have more to say to an apple tree than to a tea-time visitor.
87. Indoors or out, whatever the weather, our skirts are hemmed with dirt.
88. Our right hands are our whip hands; our left, our bridle hands. Ladies ride on the left to steel ourselves against inexpressible pleasure.
89. Self-sacrifice is the truest womanly virtue.
90. Our brains have been weighed and measured, naturally selected, which accounts for where we find ourselves, at the bottom of the tree.
91. Our greatest function is to praise.
92. We stink of peonies rotting between our legs.
93. Though we dabble, we can't tell where 'now' lives, in any language – *maintenant, adesso, jetzt*.

94. We are all context, accident, fate and don't even know it.
95. We are not ourselves.
96. We have been in mourning long enough.
97. Though we are meek, we will not inherit the earth, not a single grain.
98. What we'll leave behind is what keeps us alive.
99. Our names taken from us, taken in vain.
100. If we could, we'd say *Stop. Listen. Begin again.*

October: Samhain

We want to look up where sky's sieved through the topmost branches but must keep our eyes on our feet so we don't slip on mossy steps cut out of rock a hundred and fifty years ago. Behind the ticking of a robin we hear their voices, all those who walked here before us, who travelled with them, who travelled alone. A ribbon of lemon and bergamot leads us up and up and round and down to the clearing where the tarn hides itself beneath a blistered skin of lily pad and needle.

They are going boating where now there is no boat, no summerhouse where they'll take tea. We might sit on the wooden bench next to the cold charcoal burner, and look down the tarn's length, reaching back into… not history exactly but something like it.

Ready to stride again, we are surprised the path weaves a circle, then not surprised. Shawl or noose, it takes us down beyond the level of our own hearing, into a dark silence. For what might be seconds, minutes or perhaps an hour, we walk round and round, not knowing which way is North, lost even to ourselves.

Until a purple arrow nudges us back onto familiar terrain and we feel the weight in our hips and legs, abandon ourselves to our idea of home's magnetic force. Boots heavy with mud, we sense we are returning. How many we bring with us, invite across the threshold, have no choice now but to call our own.

We, the Dead

Seeing them approach, the tall one
is crying, the other is listening.
We await their arrival.

Trees centuries old – avenue dark
with the clutch of leaves.
The women walking comfort us.

Above our heads, and theirs, sky,
pigeon grey, swallows itself.
We hear its bones cooing.

As they draw close, everything
bleeds into something else.
The two women lose their edges.

Dizzy, we sway – lured
by the flare of their beauty.
They show us who we are.

One of us stands on her own –
hands loose, earth slipping
through her fingers,

mouth open, as if about to speak.

Morralee Wood

Moss

We won't be told who we are – clamp
 our hands over our ears and sing.
  We are fringe and tassel, patchwork

of quilts stitched with our own fingers
 and thumbs. We make ourselves over
  and over, starting again every day.

Flagpoles for the wormed and the winged –
 is that what we are? Doll's house figures?
  The world's smallest ladders to heaven?

Fallen stars? O we are thousands!
 Our code encrypted, low to the ground.
  Light comes and goes, a tarnished spoon.

Gall

We find ourselves blind, invaded, injured
   and so grow strange and outlandish,
      spit out a gob of crabbed twigs –

a witch's broom – make room for the uninvited.
   Say it's evolution: how we work round time,
      beside it, despite it. Prey to parasites

elbowing for survival, puckered and rusted,
   we sprout horns, pustules, spark spangles,
      knuckled cones. Say it's penetration:

how we're sucked dry and poisoned. Our fruit
   the apple – our bastards, twisted,
      streaked with their fathers' sins.

Burr

This land's got its hooks in us. Nowhere
   else to go. Seed, flower and fruit –
      the curse of metaphor, curse

of words black as lead. Falsehood, scandal.
   Our hair stands on end. The stain
      of bad blood saddens our clothes.

We grow on disturbed soil and replenish it,
   mend ourselves. We do not pretend
      to know where we are going,

carry our medicine in the same purse
   we keep our wounds. Brazen, inventive,
      we open ourselves to the horizon.

December: Winter Solstice

A short flight of stone steps takes us up to a line of yew trees dusted with pale yellow pollen – an augury of light. The track widens as it rises into what would have been the carriageway leading up to the Hall. What was an approach would also have been an escape, the chance to walk out of the house into the wild. The slippage on the bank means the paths are tricky to negotiate, their unevenness aggravated by a slick coating of coppery leaves. The gradient sharpens alongside a sweep of fenced-off parkland. Horses graze, jacketed creatures who look like their dreams have been stolen.

We know how they feel, fingers burning with cold, summer deleted from the camera so there's room to photograph the Cedar Hut. Inside, a book, substantial as an old family bible, appears to be growing from a rustic table. More coffin than book, the lifted lid reveals a sheaf of laminated pages.

A photograph of a woman in a frock of indeterminate colour with a tiered trim not unlike the layered shingles of the hut roof: her right hand holding a book open on her taffeta lap. Her left elbow rests on another book, her hand lifted to her chin; an expression blanked out by the time it took to catch.

The year's midnight is cold as the grave, dead wood riddled with holes. We have to keep moving, into and out of the rain. Fungi are candles guttering in the dark, lichen like frosted tongues. *Danger of Further Landslips*. We can't trust the ground under our feet; the bank falling abruptly away to the water far below, even icier than the wind scoring creases in our faces.

For a moment sunlight pierces the drizzle and every single droplet of water is suffused with light. St. Lucy's light. We walk towards it gratefully. Turning back, our path is clearly a drawing near, something more than we ahead of us.

Signs of Erosion

Earth inmost, we're slip-
shod sluts, sibyls stripped
of our proper fingertips,

feet bleeding, slippered
in glass. The gorge drips
in our throats, our hips –

daemon/double: lips
usurp us; land, scarp/scape,
drops away. Mud sticks.

[A verse here is lost.]

Gorge

Wading upriver
risking brash water
for where torrents meet
we pay no heed
to rumour, play counter to
the rules. Our snakes draw us up.
Against the heft of us
the muscular current
its tang of iron
spawns the power and fury
inside us. We will plunge
through white spray
this privileged view
gorge rising
blue gash of sky
brindled fish swept seawards
backwash of pearls.
Beware the flash
of our Medusa stare.
Beware, we well up.

Botanical Emblem | *Snowdrop*

    First flower, the strongest   *Galanthus nivalis*
(though it appears to acquiesce) –
       hymen or hood, spathe at its back.   *February fairmaids*

    Calyx: a bead milky petals   *Candlemas bells*
spring from – three, inner, pinned
       at the hub with honied gold.   *Snow piercer*

      Nectar code blazed across   *Dingle dangle*
virgin snow on a stem of pure
      longing – the smallest bulb.   *Mary's taper*

II
PROPERTY

Girlhood

§

Above the eight-sided lake she's red kite
and the lace of a daytime moon, winter
sky. She is far from herself, then incredibly
near, small as a faun, disguised as bark, grazing
the woodland floor. She forgets how he smells,
her father who art in Connecticut.
One of the 50 things no one mentions.
Every pattern is a flower or a leaf.
The touch of things she wants to touch. Pony.
Apple. Earth. At the end of the Hollow Walk –
a Column to Liberty. Her body,
an arrow carried by the wind from the sea
past Cut Thorn Farm, Fellside, up to Bird Hill.

§

Her house, home – your mother, the palindrome.
Your little shoes tapping to her tunes, she
chooses the colour of your ribbons.
One favourite, yellow – witch hazel tassels
sprung awake by innocence, a year called new.
Climbing laddered shadows on Warren Haugh
and never coming to the end of yourself –
call it more than a game – building bolt holes
from larch boughs and birch brush, conspiratorial,
breath breaking at your feet, tiny knuckles
of aconite. Your first flowers. Two cranes
on a blue china plate, always fly back
to each other, one at nine o'clock, one three.

§

As if the hill were a velvet cushion,
the folly rests on top, a crown, Gothick,
crocketed. We must cross the stone threshold
to enter the circle, hearts illuminated
by branching stars. Gathered at the table,
in the mirrors to the north and the south
of us, we are thousands, we are endless –
a murmuration of girls on the cusp
of a design we don't understand, and
won't. Even afterwards when we collect
our scattered parts – husks, chimeras, half-
forgotten hopes stirred by a wild fragrance,
the repeating curve of petal or leaf.

[*The catastrophe of a daughter was a bore, but what can't be cured must be endured and never mentioned.*]

Pedigree

Come, let us discuss those whiskery men
of invention, men of ideas, to whom
we'll build wigwams; our dreams epic, vast.

> Dressed up, we are guinea fowl, empresses,
> sapphired and rubied, crowns cresting our claws.
> The hems of our dresses are without doubt.
> They are Strathmore worsted, on Mama's side,
> lately, related to the Queen. Our doggies and we
> belong to the same tribe, well-bred, heroic,
> quick as north waters, plush-tongued. Strangers
> to self-pity and her dirty petticoats,
> our minds are our own, brook no invaders.

Tell us – that anonymous author
of *Ivanhoe*. We have heard a whisper.

White Birch and Blackthorn

We tell ourselves
we're not alone. Tell us
we're not alone.

[Norse proverb, cross stitch on linen –
In every woman there is a queen.
Speak to the queen and the queen will answer.]

Matrimony

Always, our 'beloved husband'.
(In pencil we label his bundled letters.)
His family carry history in their veins,
their battle cry *Truth! Tory! Wisdom!*
Our honeymoon, tartan and oatmeal.
He calls us, *ssh*, our secret name.
A great galloper, hunter
of flesh, fish, fowl – we stay at home.
He always makes sure the phaeton is fixed,
the chaise in perfect order.
He writes letters in haste, forgets to finish them
but supplies us with his complete itinerary.
His tenderest words say yes, he *also*....
He can dance till two in the morning.
He always knows the time.
He buys a house to call our own.
Charms our mother – she calls us her babes in the wood
(a picture of her in a locket, next to our skin).
He does his duty at the hustings and supports the best man.
He is our best man.
What we do we do for him.
He is nothing if not partial to a mutton chop.
He canvasses the county on horseback.
He has pistols and knows how to use them.
He does not always come home at nights.
He never uses the word barren.
He isn't jealous of our dogs.
One day after dinner, he makes provision in his will.
Like his mother, he wants everything correct.
One night after dinner, he dies in our arms.
Widow, a key that opens the heaviest doors.
He is everywhere we look.

February: Imbolc

All that's left of *her* Ridley Hall is the west wing – a modest structure of pale dressed stone, with an arched stable block and, inside, narrow corridors and winding stairs, the warm soapsud smell of laundry. Hanging on one wall, a pencil sketch of the Georgian building skirted by a footpath and feathery conifers. The strokes are naïve, childlike – drawn by someone whose hand couldn't always do her eyes' bidding. Small-paned windows to let the light in and a wide stand of chimney pots to keep the cold out. A fat-bellied bow window anchoring the house on the east lawn.

In the wood-panelled hallway, part-ship, part-chapel, a great bronze bell hangs. It's tempting to set it ringing to wake the dead, summon those who loved this place back to their part in the story. There are things we want to know, gaps to be filled.

Outside, we lift our heads to catch the mirabelle in blossom, wide-eyed on dark stems. We kneel to inspect hairy bittercress, chew its mustardy leaves. Greenhouses and polytunnels are waiting for spring to start their motors again. Edging the parkland, an avenue of limes tufted at the base with twiggy thickets are dense habitations for this place's restless spirits.

On our way back down the hill, we lose our compass, can't decide if the Scarlet Elf Cup, as effective as a traffic light in making us halt, is a lucky charm or a bad omen, poisonous or good to eat.

Hurricane

with a woman's name no one sees
hurtling across livid waters

till it's too late and the lid's off...
Words and selves splintered,

toppling; like particles of dust,
settle. Not 'like dust', dust.

A wild grief. Widow's weeds.

    Abandonment.

White against leaf litter, a single bone...

rib of a house some soul used to be
tenant of, keel of a wrecked boat.

Where it was attached – absence,
a faceted disc, and written there:

How to seed our own weather?

Rue d'Angoulême

What is small survives by vanishing –
moth, say, or beetle. We did it in Paris,
city of enlightenment, exile,
the guillotine. *En plein air*, her wide
avenues could hide us, while at home
locusts clustered over land and cash,
wrangled last wills and testaments –
every farthing we knew ourselves by
in question. Our disappearing act
kept us from madness. O heliotrope,
bloom of nostalgia! Baudelaire,
a decade later, chose the same street
as camouflage, inked his lines in light
among the old city's broken shadows.

[...HIS DOMESTIC VIRTUES ENDEARED HIM MORE
ESPECIALLY TO HIS DEEPLY AFFLICTED WIDOW, SUSAN
HUSSEY ELIZABETH DAVIDSON, WHO HAS CAUSED THIS
MONUMENT TO BE ERECTED IN HIS MEMORY.]

Revêtements

Our favourite seat, striped silk – oyster,
Prussian blue; stitch by stitch, our second skins,
the mahogany they hang in, our various
renderings; those best earrings, diamond and opal;

all our books, wonderlands unfurled, pages
foxed... disappeared. The furniture of our lives,
our disguises, our revêtements, all gone.

Rising, unmoored, we could land lighter;
look somewhat longer at our rooms, letters –

catch, in blown glass, a ghost's gaze.

Room Outdoors

Returning from high walls
        where we knew no peace,
we enter the dark field.

Night leans in and holds
our shoulders with such gentleness
        we shiver awake.

Beneath the belly of a bear,
the warrior's belt, eyes
        slaked on the scaffolding

        (which is no scaffolding)
of impartial stars, we are
recalibrated – significant

and inconsequential as pine cones
        in the plantation
the crescent moon

        blinks and weeps over.
Isn't this where we must dwell,
this looking: eyes naked,

short-sighted; hearts open
        to skylines we didn't choose.

March: Spring Equinox

How can the first day of spring have so much winter in it? Among tufts of wild garlic and tight-shut daffodils, snow persists. Half of us looks forward, half looks back.

Climbing the gorge, we count the steps, each flex of ankle and calf – 61, 62, 63; the last five, exposed roots worn to a graphite sheen under our boot soles. We step over them and the sharp shadows cast by sun glancing from the west; above and below, the same patterns – a tracery of veins – our own bodies made transparent.

The lie of the land transformed by snowmelt and sideways light, we stumble upon a swampy glade we've never seen before. Trees in a dream, beech and birch rise from glass, ice blooming around illuminated trunks. At the far edges, the surface clears; a mirror for tangled branches and the intense cobalt of a midday sky. Everything's the wrong way up, glittering; a door into what matters now, here, after the long huddle of winter. Eyes closed, we link hands.

We aren't dreaming the juicy new smell in the air, or the way the light falls with more mirth on our faces. On the tip of our tongues something is beginning, opening our lips and teeth and throat. What was choked can start to breathe again.

Though slower than we'd like. Below, the river's rushing with thaw, but one big stone in the middle is still covered in a clump of snow like white moss on its north side, stubborn, alive – the pagan music of cold that plays in our bones.

Second Nature

Carrying all our mothers inside
us, the burden is heavy. We find

ways to make life light enough
to bear, call ourselves lucky –

>we are many, we are few.

Only when death shows her hand
can we fight for the right to steward

our own estates, re-order our fates.
Second nature,

>this habit of making do.

Disguised in black, we turn
our backs on death and her angels,

keep faith with our vision
of staircases, hacked out of rock,

>where we'll practise the scales
>of the gorge with our boots.

Botanical Emblem | *Marsh Marigold*

Boots, brave bassinets, bullflower, bull's eyes,
cow lily, crazy Beth, crowfoot, drunkards,
golds, goldes, goldings, gools, horse blob, kingcup,
leopard's foot, mare's blob, marsh marigold,
Marybuds, Marygold, May blob, meadow-bright,
meadow buttercup, meadow cowslip,
meadow gowan, meadow routs, publicans-
and-sinners, publican's cloak, soldier's buttons,
Solsequia, *Sponsa solis*, water boots,
water bubbles, water buttercup,
water cowslip, water dragon, water
goggles, *Verrucaria*, yellow gowan –
Caltha palustris, 'goblet of the marsh' –
drowned shadows, names lost, mumbling ghosts.

III
HER CONSTANT PLEASURE TO ADORN AND BEAUTIFY

Revolution

Early on we saw how often there were circles –
moon and flower, phaeton wheels, our crinolines,
summerhouse, a felled tree, its rings, calendar,

bracelet. We inspected them on our bodies – wrist,
waist, iris, nipple, mole, the constellation we touched
at night when we were alone, and where it took us.

We sensed them cycling through our lives, their orbit –
four seasons, the clockface, those spheres assigned us
we submitted to or ached to escape from:

rabbit hole or hare's form, dark hollow in the ground,
like an open mouth, that cry ricocheting down
the long tunnel of our throat, unassailable light at the end.

Tarn

By now resigned to making a virtue
out of tears (as in *pairs*), tearing and being
torn – rough edges, sodden, accidental,
folded along a scar's feathered crease –
cold and marvellous, these small hands
fall open, empty, naturally inclined
to build a world out of nothing: starlight,
paper, cedar, rock, screeds of moss torn from
the shady understorey. If we cry
for ourselves, as well as for another,
what is pulled asunder by our own hand
need no longer send us into hiding.
Let these tears (as in *years*) make a tarn,
a body of water answered by willow, larch.

Not Words but Deeds

Tools should be sharpened each time
they're used, agreed, but what do we,
bookish, know about technique –
the exact grip on the rasped ash handle
that gives a pickaxe the greatest heft,
pounding this scarred gradient of rock
– not once but ten thousand times,
every day for months, to cut the steps
essential to our design, the landscape's
stark question – life's difficult lesson:
*first person plural; continuous
present; repeat, repeat, repeat.*

[*In the most absolute tranquility or in the midst of tumultuous events, in safety or danger, in innocence or corruption, we are a crowd of others.* From the Italian.]

Allen Banks Flora

Stitchwort
Stellaria holostea

Angled and straggly, we use grass
        and other stronger stuff to keep us upright.
Snapcrackers – one day we'll tell you
        about our kinship with headaches and bones.
Not besotted with that interminable indoors
        embroidery, *Poor-man's-buttonhole*,
we have the knack of dash in a jacket, know
        how to slacken the stitch in your side.
Between us, *Greater* and *Lesser* – a stash
        of twin-lobed stars, pocketsful of earth –
we provoke thunder, call down lightning.

Wood sorrel
Oxalis acetosella

We are salad and mystical, swinging
        to and fro between sorrow and alleluia.
We offer up our threefold origami hearts
        like someone casting all their luck
away for those who crave to be free
        of melancholy (though not too much
for they would sorely miss it).
        Here we sleep, beauties, drooping
on moss cushions strewn over fallen logs.
        Granny's sour grass, here we are, yes,
and no one comes – not even to eat us.

Sun spurge
Euphorbia helioscopia

Discs ahoy to look at the sun, we shine
      as bright, though we cling to the edges.
Like our sisters, *Dwarf* and *Petty*,
      our inflorescence is a shallow cup big
enough for male and female, a ring
      of horned glands. We consider ourselves
uncommon, discuss matters scientific
      with physicians, the ichneumon wasp.
Ants also love us. In autumn, we'll crack
      like rifles scattering seeds – a method
borrowed by Miss Gertrude Jekyll.

Ivy-leaved toadflax
Cymbalaria muralis

Other names, better in our opinion –
    Mother of Thousands, Madonna Flower,
for we travelled here from Italy: we sun
    ourselves against red brick in the kitchen garden.
What it is to be hairless and sprawling,
    quaintly languishing! Mauve snapdragons,
yellow pouts lean towards the light
    and when they harden to seed, we switch
on a sixpence and squeeze ourselves
    among crumbling alkali to overwinter. Bravo!
We clap our little hands like cymbals.

[Applause.]

May: Beltane

When trees are brought down in a storm, their roots are upended, exposed, losing their rootishness to become shoulder and fox and mountain and belovèd. The rockface along the gorge is also open to revision. If we look long enough, we see what is old is new, what is hard is soft, grey is all colours and cold is warm. We must keep climbing.

Ferns give birth to themselves. Antediluvian fiddleheads playing a tune we no longer dance to. Papery scales on taut stems – spines on a dinosaur's back, a pterodactyl's raggedy wings. Their heads are coiled, thinking about springing, thinking about brown turning into green, fretting the air.

We say leaves as if they were one thing but they are many, each different to another. Blue-green, brown-green, yellow-green, grey-green. Green sliding off the edge of green. We love you, little green.

As high as we can go, a young duck and drake make a waterborne promenade the length of the tarn, dipping and swallowing as they glide. Sometimes he leads and she follows; when she changes direction, he's not far behind. They forage on the margins and on dry land stop to groom themselves, keeping a polite distance; their necks elastic. After sharing a few low croaks, they lift their wings and speed down the watery runway – in perfect tandem, take flight.

Pedometers for Ladies

Mr Payne (Inventor) has instructed us
his Patent Pedometer needs <u>no</u> <u>winding</u> <u>up</u>
at any time. When we commence walking
we must set the Hand exactly on the Twelve
and keep his Device suspended by the Hook
on a Riband round our Neck so the figures
on the Dial-plate show by the pointing
of the Hand the number of Miles we walk.
The four dots are Quarters. We follow
his Directions. For our guidance: No 1
is the Pedometer as it is worn.
No 2 shows the wheels beneath the Dial.
No 3 is the Pendulum and Regulator.
Mr Payne (& Co) is our Obedient Servant.

Unrelated

Sisters are awkward as knives
that don't match laid on the table

but sometimes the clatter of cutlery
is what we need – nickel-plating, tarnish,

no brother telling us what we must do or
think or be. Here we be. We lock eyes.

Trade each other's pasts, our torn places,
stainless river stitching us together.

Or we lose each other, out of blindness.

Some, not sprung from the same seed,

our eyes different colours, sit
and look at the view till it's lodged inside

us, holds us to its original moment.
The whole summer we spend dreaming

like this. Sometimes of each other,
our many-coloured eyes.

Sometimes knives.

In Praise of the View Across the Valley (Obscured Now by Trees)

With the chalet's eaves and leaded panes behind us,
we thought ourselves planted in an Alpine setting,
edelweiss stars enchanting the mountain,
where thin air smelled of snow and the fur of goats;
the horizon high, a glass half-full, level
with our eyes. The sun was lit beeswax
on the chandeliers of the larches. Distant fields
suggested brocade; the whole view, maybe a ballroom –
in a palace – in Switzerland – on the slopes
of the Matterhorn. Sitting there, we could almost hear
glass tinkling, fans swishing, feather and silk,
the laughter that emanates from pleasure, skin
and bone pleasure, not just people pretending,
fooling nobody, not even themselves.

Written in the Dark

I is icicle,
transparently exact,
entirely temporary.
Can't write with that.

Y is copperplate hook
slung there and back
across perpendicular lines.
Yours truly.

> The lie of I unselves us.
> We deserve more of you.

[Ink running out, fingerprints.]

sketch for a sonnet, unattributed

without which we think we
cannot address each other
in or with or from love
as if it is love's nature to be
a transaction personal individual
though we can expect nothing
back except this blood we carry
inside us like a wild river
we build bridges across
to get to where we want to be
and between us never find
a single route or return with
only our dogs lifting their noses
into our hands able to console us

To Squire Bruno of Ridley Hall

*You will, I am sure, be pleased to learn
that we arrived here in safety,
received a most affectionate welcome
from yr fellow Canine, excepting
he <u>omitted</u> the <u>Ceremony</u>
of <u>knocking</u> <u>one</u> <u>down</u>.
      I am induced
to trouble you, as I wish you
to execute a little Commission,
namely, to present to your mistress
the set of China she ordered
to replace sundry Charms in her Dinner Set,
doubtless you had some share in breaking –
      Had she and I been together
on the 17th I shd have spared you
this trouble, but now I request you
will negotiate for me; I have
by this post written an Order
to my Banker to transfer to her acct.
as many pounds as you have toes,
and I desire you will trot over
to H. and bring back that Sum.
      So now,
Adieu Dear Mr B.*

Excuse blots –

Bilberry Hill Moss House

In the hut there is only room for one.
Where solitude happens, don't we spend
all our time picking bones with others?
The price of too-human eyes. Everything
here is green, the colour of envy,

our heart's stain. Curved walls persuade against
comparison, help us contain ourselves
for the time being. Sheltered from the wind,
we watch it swirl an uprush of leaves.
Inside our bilberry nest, it's only natural

to assume the condition of moss,
understated, slow, primordially patient;
a tang of timelessness on the tongue
we soon find we have no use for, this round earth
keening in our stead her silent language.

[*By the kindness of the proprietor, strangers are allowed
to visit the walks after asking admission at the house.*]

Sun on the Cusp of the Bull and Twins

Save this day's gathering, the ark of us.
Weren't we always nothing

                            but earth's creatures –
hart's tongue, viper's bugloss, bear's ears, hogweed,
running wild through the shape-shifting valley,
light impossible without shade,

                            ascent
without descending

                  (if we ever want
to sprint home). We are walking with strangers
who become fellow conspirators.

        We are violets
growing on tree trunks like keepsakes;
the first cuckoo calling, our promises
tangled together – clotted weed in the tarn,
that smell of sap we pray will never end.

We're the cool of the raven's claw,
hesitation where three paths meet:
garlic – unbridled,
        crane's bill – bloody,
woodruff – sweet.
        Damselflies, their blue glint,
skating on a rink of warm air.

                            We are
the outline of our bodies in the grass
when we rise,
        the river's engine idling,
a pool deep enough to swim, the dipper
switching among roots,

                      the foam that lodges
round stones, those insects (too many to count)

glancing the water to lay their eggs.
                                        We're
caterpillars hammocked in the trees –
bird cherry, alder, our lost spindle.
We are fat white dandelions chiming
day's end –
            how different it appears now
in strong light, with all these others beside us.

The Cedar Hut
(Deconstructed)

Dipped beneath a compass
        of horizons, river spilling
down from the treeline, we inhale –
        cedrene, cedrol, widdrol,
thujospene, sesquiterpenes –
        and unwind...stripped of bark
or camouflaged with lichen,
        here inside is outside,
and vice versa, where we can
        picture difference as a place,
like this, of light, shelter,
        the liberty to exhale.

[That this evening may be holy, good and peaceful,
let us pray with one heart and mind.

Followed by a time of silence.]

Botanical Emblem |*Mountain Pansy*

Each little thought is five-petalled,
      voilà, tri-coloured, pricked and whiskered,
nobody's eyes' exact shade.

They will not be divided, resist
      being bedded and gardened; wait
in ambush past the twist in the water

where they bring folk to their knees,
      them and the orange-tip butterfly.
Saying yes or saying zero

hinges on a hidden spur, veined dust
      of purple and green. These are not
their thoughts. They are not their thoughts.

      Prescribe medicinal heartsease,
forked sorcery of love-in-idleness.

IV
THE GREATEST INTEREST IN THE WELFARE

Staffage

We are stuff, but decorative, extras
in a play, the anonymous populace
telling our storykins – plus sound effects
(cartwheel rattle) or smells (cowshit, soot).

Not much difference between human
and animal, we are anchor and icon,
kermess, capriccio. We punctuate scale,
sprung from the land itself, picturesque.

Nature and Culture align in the mass of us.
We discuss The Virtuous Life,
or its shadow, while we animate the scene,
raising the market value of landscape.

Our names, now forgotten, go as Usefulness,
Harmony, Drama. Open to interpretation.

Seedlip Girls

Knowing nothing but what's in our hands –
baskets made of reeds – we weave under and over,
around and around. They and the seeds
inside are kin among kin. And us, walking
up and down, back and forth, we scatter
measured fingerfuls. We scatter ourselves
to the day's weather, our minds on maybe,
perhaps, so the time might pass with no trouble.

Pray we don't sow the seeds of our own
trouble, swinging between hollow and stone
in our bellies, and fields unbroken beyond our ken.
Even asleep, still sowing, dreaming our arms lift
and fall. Flightless wings. Earth at our feet.
Ribbed brown rows that don't belong to us.

The Shieling

Here, where the bellflowers blow

Where winter never comes
Where we go to hide

Where we unharness our river
And breathe each other's air

Where we swathe chapped hands
      in sheep's wool

Where kissing's not the half of it

Sweet as watermint
      tamped earth

Where we are queen
And the trees all our people

[*quean*, n. a saucy girl: a woman of worthless character: a girl (Scot.) – In N.E. Scotland *queyn, quine,* dim.*queynie, quinie*, the ordinary words for a girl. O.E. *cwene*, woman (O.E. *cwen*, queen)]

June: Summer Solstice

The north wall faces south, every handmade brick taxed, and mortared to its neighbour. Three fire houses are home to shadows and cobwebs, the crackle of dried leaves. Picnic benches squat at angles among young apple trees clustered with fattening fruit. On a quiet weekday only four cars (two German, two Japanese) are parked in the bays where vegetables were raised and nurtured from seed. While we eat our lunch, we attempt a diagram of the lost rows – lettuce, spring onions, the beginnings of marrows, broad beans.

Much of the crop would have been forced by a careful hierarchy of gardeners; at the bottom, women, weeding, hoeing, picking off caterpillars. Women, always bent, the bones in their backs burning from the inside. The sound of the river behind us might be the spiked tips of their leather gloves scratching at gravel paths, hooking out anything that dared to grow there, upholding God's own order.

Our mouths are full of flies, nameless insects that catch in our throats. Hard to swallow. Too. Hot. No. Air. Under our feet, grass dizzy with buttercups, self-heal. A flight of steps rises into nowhere – the path up to the Hall, erased, nothing left but the idea.

What good will come of us singing the praises of car parks that used to be kitchen gardens and kitchen gardens that used to be car parks, adding our voices to the bees' buzz under the old roof slates – still here, still enjoying warm pollen cupped in the curves of red brickwork, sweet resplendent lime.

We fill a cotton bag with the frothy heads of elderflowers, take them home to soak with lemon and sugar for cordial. Summer stoppered in a bottle. Won't last past August.

Stonepicker

after George Clausen

She's light and wild enough yet
to have more in common with meadow flowers.

Stubborn flickers of white and bruised chicory
scissor through the grassy slope

while her grandmother, drab in sacking,
nearer my age now, is stooped, almost

on her knees, apron weighed down
with a harvest of scree and muddy limestone.

The girl's face is tender though she already
knows too much: a scarlet cloth

flares in the tumbled basket and jug.
Thin trees jut against a northern sky –

all I can do is keep on, keep on walking
towards them, and pick stones

from the furrowed page to make room
for harebell, lady's smock, three-leaf clover.

[*Bones, for instance, are mostly sold by the cook or kitchen-maid; but wherever there is a garden, not a bone ought to be allowed to leave the premises. Bone dust, pounded bones, bones in almost any shape, are essential manures for turnips, asparagus and most other culinary plants. Not only are plants grown with their aid finer to the eye but, what is better, they are more nutritious to the human system.*]

Under the Eaves

Candle's snuffed when he doesn't
knock on the oak door never locked
so when we wake up he's there
already on top of us – hard
to breathe know what to do
him pressing us and shut tight
our eyes ears throats while he prises
open all our necessary corners –
the bed soaked when he's done
no more our nest our own downie
us crying and crying and the room
listening till we hear it shush us
You'll live, like your mother
and her mother before you.
Dry those eyes now, get to work.

[*The time approaches when these soliloquies shall be shared.*
We shall not always give out a sound like a beaten gong as one
sensation strikes and then another.]

Wild Teasel

When you were green
and we were girls

we'd sip the rain
between your lips

      Now as old
as you are brown

bones worn sharp
throats blown dry

we call on you
to card the wool

that'll see us through
till we lie back down

in summer ground

Pressed Flowers

Frances
        Jane
                      Isabella
Anne   Mary   Margaret
                          Hannah
Catherine May   Elizabeth Helen
        Alice   Eleanor Ann
          Sarah   Louisa
    Ursula   Jean

                Bell
              Coulson
            Dickinson
              Dodd
             Ellison
             English
            Errington
            Ferguson
             Gibson
            Herdman
             Hume
             Lowes
            McDougall
            McEwan
            Pearson
             Prior
           Richardson
             Ridley
            Robson
            Teasdale
            Wallace
           Wilkinson
             Wilson
            Woodman

Salvage

Balancing history inside us like a bowl brimful
of water, we are beings who mourn, who know

ten times more than we could ever say, truth
thicker than any yarn we could coax through

our wheels and spin. Who'll say our names over
and over and over and over again and again,

again and again so the past will last longer
than a good winter coat? So much of us is water,

on our death bed every drop will give up the ghost,
the mist, O Lord, of our rattled breath.

Mirrors draped in shawls or turned to the walls.

[N.B. *Once we can no longer speak for ourselves, we are interpreted.
...history is not the past – it is the method we have evolved of
organising our ignorance of the past.*]

Lapidary

We have no centre.　　　　　We are the centre
from which all earth radiates　　　mica tucked
in our crevices　　　　the forgottenness of things.
We break open　　　near, far　　　crowbone
ash　　　　carapace of the soul. There
is nowhere to go.　　　　　How should we ask
permission to enter　　　　our own home?
Made from mud　　　　　lichen, dust
a woman's touch　　　　　housewifely we wipe
away　begin again.　　　　From before
history happened　　　　　our hands reach out.
Here we are　　　　a constant recurrence
strata　mauve, ochre　　　　given to endure.

[*Written originally in the Language of Nature,
(of later Years but little understood).*]

Botanical Emblem | *Throatwort*

Flicked back at the lip, a scattering of bells
      that don't ring – cast from such underthings
as womany linen worn thin
      and suggestible with their monthly
laundering: if this flower were a maiden, how
      she'd be chimed by a gobbet of flies, longhorns
and bees who couldn't get enough,
      scouring crown, then waist, then mouth
            to soft white silence.

V
IN
REMEMBRANCE
OF

Mighty, Far-springer, Queen

Gorge-dwellers, overlooked in the dark –
rock and buckle, ravel and cleave –
we are spliced.
Blood from our right flank sparks the dead back
to life. From our left, it can kill
a man walking.
This is how we're finished, our endless refrain.
Fast-skinned and weathering, apotropaic,
our eyes shiver
fools to stone. Will we always be this transparent,
tempered with claw and tusk, scale and wing?
Held up as bolt
or sanction, screening the underworld's dank
threshold? We give birth to mares,
gorgeous serpents.

Unnatural

Hard to say when, or how, it happened.
Alone with the mirror, where our lips

used to be, nothing reflected back –
the not-there pallor of a corpse.

Friends' mouths became blanched echoes:
almonds surrendering skins; embroidery

unpicked; mucky linen scrubbed clean. Soon
all our lips were white, Madonna lilies.

Words, unwritten, unspoken – opposite
happiness – ghosts of what might have been.

None of the men seemed to notice (at least
it was never mentioned) so we thought –

of course! – our imagination, light
playing tricks. Drained of blood, our faces

stayed sealed. Abstractions. Ill omens.
All we could reveal was our fatigue.

August: Lughnasa

From up here our horizon is imported from Rome – road, wall and border. A line of pylons sutures wounded latitudes. Purple streaks of heather on the downward slope set bees buzzing at the back of the brain, a drip of honey, strong and dark.

An acid green field is L-shaped, flecked with what could be daisies but we know to be sheep. A glimpse of lorries on the A69 – east to west and west to east – passing inspection signs that say, in order: *Whitechapel, Little Bridge, Lipwood Bridge, Lipwood Retaining Wall, South Tyne Viaduct, East Land Ends, Cemetery Road, Gees Wood, Crossley Burn, Coastley, Kingshaw Green, Constantius, Birkey Burn, Hermitage Bridge, Hermitage.* As we drive back and forth, following our own desire lines, burning our own bridges, we pass these signs too. The names sing in our heads.

We have to look long and far because, from this bench, precisely arranged for a view of the Hall, the middle distance is eclipsed by self-seeded saplings of birch and oak. We resist the imprint of privilege, but without the paths *she* made through the woodland, her lines of desire, we wouldn't have found our way.

Above the skyline, contrails draft an aerial map of the roads, intersecting and dissolving before our eyes. Somewhere to the left of us, half a mile away, a peacock cries.

Feverish Note

Must begin with hopes and wishes.
Outdoors, hard showers and thunder –
the weather sadly has been against us.

We long to see our <u>especial</u> <u>darlings</u>.
Another storm threatens – wild terror!
Don't forget our hopes and wishes.

Afforded indeed the greatest pleasure...
Racking cough, want of sleep, sciatica.
Sadly, the weather's been against us.

Most affectionately attached, we persist –
pray do not trouble – no formal order.
~~Untillegible~~ hopes and wishes.

O Shame. These clouds must burst.
Forgive – inflamed eye, throat sore.
Must conclude with hopes and wishes
though the weather sadly stays against us.

Blank

When we were ___, we were
rarely overlooked, nothing ___
about their attention: ___, ___.
___, our faces were mercury.
We often didn't ___ what to do
with our hands or ___. They'd soon
direct us and we had ___ choice.
Is that why we felt ___, disinclined
to hold their gaze, our own core.

Now we are ___, we are
generally ignored, as if we were ___,
not just empty, excised, ___ taken
to the nth degree, ___ distilled
to homeopathic potency, not even
a placebo, ___, elided, demeaned.
We can't articulate this ___.
Walls, floors, ceilings, doors all ___
so we staunch each other's ___ and rise.

[*We do not recollect how we disposed of ourselves.*]

Memorandum
(Found Among Our Papers)

Witchcraft
*Snowdrop**Misfortune*
–
*Overthrew Lords**Shoe*

Cards

Button
*–**One Eye*
Maypole
*The other half**That which it eats*

Curfew

*Circumbendibus**because it is half stuff*
Wainscot
*Washbale**Glove*
The letter S
19 days
*–**991*
*The –**99*
Cough

Hair
*Portrait**Mandate*
Onion

Magnet
Currants
*Pleasure**Map of the World*

63 & 45

4 Cats

Level
Dictionary

Foxglove
Mourning Ring
Turnpike
Card table
Needle
I
Adriatic
Ten
Evil
Father
Hose
Checkmate
Counterfeit
Because they come
after I

China, blue and white

We rescue muddy notes
sent by our grandmothers

from soil that swallows
soil that rots:

>　　*your plates and cups*
>　　*already broken*

glaze veined
with grains of dirt

archivists of our own lives
do we save ourselves

from ourselves
hands turning blue

bones showing through
clay born from earth

gone back to earth
cast away

where is it –
this *away*?

Self-Portrait as a Collective Noun

Our edges all a-tremble like the ring
round a below-zero moon, where do we
begin? Point to the quarter where we end.
If one catch-all for our loose assembly
is *bevy*, who imagined us 'ladies'

larks, quails, swans, maybe roes, powder-puff
scuts vanishing among dry winter brush?
It cracks and shakes in our wake. No escape
from this fenced-off place we ran to, gathered
for safety, unable to drink our fill.

Coup de Théâtre

Finding Granny's Bonnets and Chinese Parasols
is a night at the *Varieties*, gaslit stage
hissing with villains – the Amethyst Deceiver
and Slippery Jack, Destroying Angels all.

Our grandmothers, cast as Primrose-gilled Rushulas,
Milk Caps, Blushers, whether through vanity, lust
or doubt, are seduced by Stinkhorns and Tough Shanks.
Our flesh crawls: that is the Sickener. Candlesnuff.

Earth Tongues fall silent. Puffballs smoke. Until the Grey
can be trounced, the Miller – White Knight – enter stage right
(a grove of oak) and fight a duel to the Death Cap.

The happy ending's frilled with False Chanterelles;
our starstruck lips glittery Brackets of toxic spores.

Plenitude

Dear reader, what we are recording
is a diaspora, not an empire.
We go deep as well as wide; sing
anthems of our ancestors, divided
no more into damned and saved.
The calendar of our flesh crimsons
our reiver names, forges a chain.
River's a mirror, the land inside us.

Our plot of earth is a borrowed book
begun in sunshine, finished in hail.

Blood. Breath. How light cascades.

September: Autumn Equinox

We almost don't find what's left of the knucklebone floor from her vanished moss house, obscured as it is by beech mast, soil and snapped twigs, fallen leaves. Down on our knees, we clear it, sweep the space clean and articulate the circumference with scraps of wood. We could be mourners tending a grave, marking the limits of what isn't there.

More than half-buried, the bones are hollowed rings and curls, grey worn to white in places, with tiny holes. All that remains of living, breathing beasts, traces of collagen and calcium. Remember the diagnosis: *It is a joy to be hidden but a disaster not to be found.*

Above, beech bark has been gouged by Dan and Leanne, Kenzy, Rat and Bear, with others who felt compelled to cut their names, leave something of themselves behind. Those of a different persuasion do the opposite – take something away with them, pine cone or tutsan leaf, acorn or weathered quartz. A souvenir of one day in one place: *We were here.* Taking what is given and what isn't, breathing in and breathing out, against the odds, various translations of we, and our bones, survive.

No/Return

    When an acorn falls, it sounds
   the world's ending. Ruthless,
flawed, we flit round

    in circles – dragonflies,
   fretted bronze, grazing
a tarn's ambiguous margins.

    Distant guns blast holes
   through the canopy of spore
and wrensong. In autumn's thrall,

    are we lost or found? Drawn back
   and back to this water, its trick
of the dark – how deep, still unclear.

For Those Unborn

If we are snakes eating our own tails,
forgive us – we know not what we do.
Eyes on a new conclusion, there is no

end: from here, the ouroboros view

is a hollow circle, a paradise starved
on its own excess. In your name,
what if we listen now to the quiet ones,

the dead ones, hold what's broken

as if it were flesh of our own flesh –
even though we bleed. What if we open
our red hands to you, let fall what falls.

Hoop-la! We must learn to love thee.

Winding Sheet

In the end nothing
on our lips but
yew, yew, yew.

[*The round cry of round being makes the sky round
like a cupola. And in this rounded landscape,
everything seems to be in repose.*]

Flock

    Eyes of heaven,

we are bird, shadow of bird,
all the souls that ever lived,
        the dead all around you.
We articulate air,
perfect circles,
     surrender to nothing.
Our language is flock
is flying is falling,
       hearts uncaged, calling.
What words can find
where beauty lives,

count the cost
of liberty?

We build our homes
with no corners,
        nests in clouds –
more space for seeing
what's true all around us.

We'll teach you
how to plummet,
      defer to gravity,
the grave's horizon,
how letting go's more

about love than dying –
spiralling.
        When it's time

we fly north, leave
only bones, a dream

of feathers, more light
than you can bear,

this small planet
                      your heart

                                        pitching

Heartland

Not long after we say it's there
and steer towards it, the world's winds
scupper our compass till next time

we catch a hint of a shiver
of a whisker of a cypher, a husk
of a heartbeat – home – here – these – stars.

Botanical Emblem | *Black-Eyed Susan*

Now you see we,
>Now you don't. We
Are ghost. We
>Are les autres, you, we.

Heed the heft of we,
>Bloody cleft of we.
Left bereft, we
>Keen for we.

Eyes black, we
>Redact lack of we
So you regard we
>Illuminated: *WE*.

Lit flower of we,
>Bitten fruit of we,
Resurrect we.
>*Gloriosa.*

Notes and References

['By quotation she sought to rob history of its power over women.' Jane Marcus, 'Thinking Back Through Our Mothers' (1981)]

SAPIENTER SI SINCERE – 'Wisely if Sincerely', the Davidson family motto – on the memorial to Susan Hussey Elizabeth Jessup Davidson in St Cuthbert's Church, Beltingham, Northumberland.

A Hundred Ways to Know Our Place – Hannah More (1745–1833) also wrote: 'It is a fundamental error to consider children as innocent beings, whose little weaknesses may perhaps want some correction, rather than as beings who bring into the world a corrupt nature and evil dispositions, which it should be the great end of education to rectify.' *Strictures on the Modern System of Female Education* (1799).

A verse here is lost – from Aeschylus's *The Suppliant Women*, around 470 BCE.

Gorge – gorge, *n.* the throat: a ravine: the entrance to an outwork (*fort.*): a hawk's crop: the maw: the contents of the stomach: a gluttonous feed: a fish-catching device, to be swallowed by the fish. – *v.t.* to swallow greedily: to glut. – *v.i.* to feed gluttonously. – *adj.* gorged having a gorge or throat: glutted: having a crown or coronet about the neck (*her.*). – *n.* gorget a piece of armour for the throat: a metal badge formerly worn on the breast by army officers: a wimple: a neck ornament. – have one's gorge rise to be filled with loathing; heave the gorge to retch. [O.Fr.] Gorgon – *n.* one of three fabled female monsters (Stheno, Euryale, and Medusa), of horrible and petrifying aspect, winged, with hissing serpents for hair: (usu. without *cap.*) anybody, esp. a woman, very ugly or formidable. [Gr. *Gorgo*, pl. *-ones* – *gorgos*, grim.]

Botanical Emblem – emblem, *n*. a picture representing to the mind something different from itself: a symbolic device or badge: a type or symbol: an inlaid ornament (*Milt.*). [L., – Gr. *emblema, -atos*, a thing inserted – *en*, in, and the root of *ballein*, to throw.]

Girlhood – Susan Davidson grew up at Gibside (now a National Trust property in Tyne & Wear). The estate was owned by her uncle, John Bowes, the 10th Earl of Strathmore. She and her mother and sister lived in Bird-hill House. The Column to Liberty, erected by Susan Davidson's great-grandfather, was second only in height to the Monument to the Great Fire of London.

The catastrophe of a daughter – Lady Westminster, on giving birth to her eighth daughter in 1834. Joan Perkin, *Victorian Women* (1993).

Matrimony – In 1830 John Davidson bought Ridley Hall and its estate at Allen Banks, Northumberland, where he already had family connections, as a home for himself and his wife Susan. It was gifted to the National Trust by Francis Bowes-Lyon (1856–1948) in 1942.

Rue d'Angoulême – Susan Davidson stayed at No.17 between March and July 1845. Baudelaire stayed at No.18 between January and June 1856. In 1846 Susan Davidson stayed for three months at 3 Rue Méromesniel.

HIS DOMESTIC VIRTUES – memorial to John Davidson Esquire (1797–1842) in St Cuthbert's Church, Beltingham.

Room Outdoors – 'Entrapped in being, we shall always have to come out of it. And when we are hardly outside of being, we always have to go back into it. Thus, in being, everything is circuitous, roundabout, recurrent, so much talk; a chaplet of sojournings, a refrain with endless verses.' Gaston Bachelard, *The Poetics of Space* (1958).

Not Words but Deeds – the inscription on a seal used on a letter to 'Mrs Davidson, Westgate Street, Newcastle. To be forwarded to Otterburn (...my darling Suzette)' from her 'truly affect^e mother AMJ' (Anna Maria Jessup, 1770-1832), dated 31 May 1825, Harrogate. Strathmore Estate Archives. 'Deeds not Words' was also, sometime later, the motto of the Suffragettes. It is inscribed on Emily Wilding Davison's gravestone at St Mary the Virgin in Morpeth, Northumberland.

From the Italian – 'In the most absolute tranquility or in the midst of tumultuous events, in safety or danger, in innocence or corruption, we are a crowd of others. And this crowd is certainly a blessing for literature.' Elena Ferrante, *Frantumaglia* (2016).

Applause – lifted from the conclusion of a review of a talk in a Victorian newspaper that has since proved untraceable.

Pedometers for Ladies – A letter and instructions (28th May 1851) sent on behalf of 'William Payne, Inventor, 163, New Bond Street', among Susan Davidson's correspondence, would suggest that she owned such a device. It may have proved useful for calculating distances during the layout of her landscape design.

Written in the Dark – Many of Susan Davidson's letters are written cross-wise, a technique used to save paper and postage. Once the paper is full, the letter is turned at a right angle and the writing continues over the top of the previous script. Hard to decipher, it was derided as a feminine affectation. There is a mention of 'all that chequer-work' in Jane Austen's *Emma* (1815).

By the kindness – from *A Handbook for Travellers in Durham and Northumberland*, written for John Murray by Augustus Hare, a distant cousin of Susan Davidson's. This entry continues: 'At the top of the woods, on rt. of the Allen, a grass terrace leads to *Bilberry Hill Moss House*, whence there is an extensive view up the deep glen, to the promontory which is crowned by Staward Peel. Hence, a winding-path descends to *the Raven's Crag*, a bold cliff of yellow sandstone, which overhangs the river.

A slightly built chain bridge is swung across the stream a little lower down, whence a steep path in the hill leads through the wood called the *Birkie Brae*, to a tarn in the hilltop under a grove of dark Scotch firs, and close to the purple moorland. Hence passing *the Swiss Cottage*, the *Hawk's Nest* is reached by the *Craggy Pass*, a narrow staircase cut in the side of the rocks which overhang it. Different views of the woods and of the Allen are presented at every turn of these walks (which were entirely constructed by the present owner), and the foregrounds are a mixture of grey rock, heather, and hanging-wood, with parasitic plants twining from stem to stem. The walks have lately been extended to a bold range of rocks near Plankie Mill.' *New and Revised Edition, with Travelling Map* (1873). The use of italics Hare's own.

To Squire Bruno – taken from a letter from Mary Bowes (1777–1855) to her niece Susan Davidson, December 5th 1853.

The Cedar Hut (Deconstructed) – 'That this evening may be holy, good and peaceful' – Evensong, Church of England ('Contemporary Language').

Staffage – indebted to Maja Markovic's 'Why the Little People Count: The Art of Staffage'. (Christie's). kermess – a fair in the Low Countries [Du. *kermis* – *kerk*, church, *mis*, mass.]. capriccio – a sportive motion: a species of free composition, not subject to form or figure (*mus.*) [Fr. *caprice* and It. *capriccio*; perh. From L. *caper* (m.), *capra* (f.), a goat.].

Stonepicker – George Clausen's painting *Stonepickers (Midday)*, 1882, is in the Laing Art Gallery, Newcastle. E.S. Delamer, *The Kitchen Garden; or, the culture in the open ground of roots, vegetables, herbs and fruits* (1855).

Under the Eaves – 'The time approaches' – Virginia Woolf, *The Waves* (1931).

Wild Teasel – The botanical name *Dipsacus fullonum* derives from the Greek 'to thirst', referring to the way rainwater collects in the cup-like structures formed round the stem by the leaf bases. This led to the plant being called 'Venus's lips' or 'Venus's basin'. The dry seedheads were used to tease out, or card, wool before spinning.

Pressed Flowers – names taken from Ridley Township Censuses of 1841, 1851, 1861 and 1871 and Beltingham Church Burials 1830-77.

Salvage – written under the influence of Hilary Mantel's 2017 Reith Lectures, *Resurrecting the Dead*, from which the following quotation also comes. And this: 'We carry the genes and the culture of our ancestors, and what we think about them shapes what we think about ourselves, and how we make sense of our time and place.'

Lapidary – 'Written originally...' – from the frontispiece of *The Adventures of EOVAAI, Princess of Ijaveo,* published anonymously in London in 1736, written by Eliza Heywood.

Mighty, Far-springer, Queen – According to Hesiod (7th century BCE), the three gorgons were Stheno, the Mighty, Euryale, the Far-springer, and Medusa, the Queen. '...one of the most potent ancient symbols of male mastery over the destructive dangers that the very possibility of female power represented. It is no accident that we find her decapitated – her head proudly paraded by this decidedly un-female female deity. There are many ancient variations on Medusa's story. One famous version has her as a beautiful woman raped by Poseidon in a temple of Athena, who promptly transformed her, as punishment for the sacrilege (punishment to her, note), into a monstrous creature with a deadly capacity to turn to stone anyone who looked at her face.' Mary Beard, *Women and Power. A Manifesto* (2017). Medusa is in a double bind: she suffers both being seen and not being seen; her own seeing is monstrous and dangerous – reflected in *Mighty, Far-Springer, Queen*'s lexicon of contronyms or 'Janus words', having contradictory meanings depending on the context.

Unnatural – *écriture feminine,* proposed by French feminist critics such as Hélène Cixous, Luce Irigaray, Julia Kristeva and Monique Wittig, has been called 'writing in white ink', the text invisible on a white page.

Feverish Note – all lines found in Susan Davidson's letters, dated 1871. Her '<u>especial</u> <u>darlings</u>' refer to John and Joséphine Bowes' dogs, much-loved by Susan Davidson. Bowes Museum Archive.

Blank – An accidental echo can be heard in the report that 'a friend of Lady Stanley of Alderney told her in 1859 that her life "would be a blank" if her pregnancy did not result in the birth of a boy.' Joan Perkin, *Victorian Women* (1993). 'We do not recollect how we disposed of ourselves' – 15 March 1798, *The Journals of Dorothy Wordsworth*.

Memorandum – in the handwriting of Mary Bowes, Susan Davidson's 'excellent aunt'. Undated.

Self-Portrait as Collective Noun – see Denise Riley's *Am I That Name? The Category of 'Women' in History* (1988); bevy, *n.* a company or flock of larks, quails, swans, roes, or ladies. [Origin obscure.]

September: Autumn Equinox – 'It is a joy to be hidden but a disaster not to be found.' – D.W. Winnicott, *Playing and Reality* (1971).

Winding Sheet – the etymology of 'yew' is variously recorded as originating from the Ancient Greek for 'arrow' or the Celtic 'ivin' or Greek 'hyfe' for cloth. Chambers emphasises its connection being rather with 'bows' and adds 'yew twigs regarded as emblematic of grief'.

The round cry – Gaston Bachelard, *The Poetics of Space*. Bachelard also quotes Jules Michelet, *L'Oiseau* (1856): 'The bird, which is almost completely spherical, is certainly the sublime and divine summit of living concentration. One can neither see, nor even imagine, a higher degree of unity. Excess of concentration, which constitutes the great personal force of the bird, but which implies its extreme individuality, its isolation, its social weakness.'

Botanical Emblem | Black-Eyed Susan – *Rudbeckia hirta*'s 'common' name is Black-Eyed Susan. Gardener Dan Pearson calls them Gloriosa Daisies. This poem borrows the form of Gwendolyn Brooks's 'We Real Cool' (1960).

Acknowledgments

I am grateful to Linda Anderson, Tara Bergin, Sinéad Morrissey, Sean O'Brien, Jacob Polley and Jo Shapcott for their generous and insightful responses to this work during my PhD *Women on the Edge of Landscape* at Newcastle University, awarded in 2020.

I also appreciated the encouragement of first readers Jo Aris, Matilda Bevan, Cynthia Fuller, Anabel Gammidge and Kim Lewis.

Many thanks to the archivists I encountered in the course of my research: June Holmes at the Natural History Society of Northumbria's Library, Great North Museum: Hancock, Liz Bregazzi and staff at Durham County Record Office, Judith Phillips at Bowes Museum, Barnard Castle, and Dan Gordon, Keeper of Biology at Great North Museum: Hancock. Also to Robert Bluck and Bardon Mill Local History Society.

Quotations from Susan Davidson's correspondence are reproduced by kind permission of Lord Strathmore and Durham County Record Office, and Bowes Museum.

Rebecca Hetherington, Chris Johnson and Mark Newman of the National Trust were helpful regarding the history of Allen Banks.

Thanks to the editors of *Butcher's Dog, dhamma moon, The Heart of the Matter, Long Poem Magazine, Poem for the North, Poetry Review* and *Ten Poems about History* for publishing some of the poems along the way.

Much gratitude to Matilda Bevan for our walks and talks at Allen Banks and beyond, and for permission to reproduce a section of her *Study of a Stream* sequence on the book's cover.

And thank you to Andy Croft for his dedicated and expansive editing at Smokestack.